To Jane,

Happy Mother's Day!

Phillis 2019

CELEBRATING

Motherhood

with the

PROPHETS

CELEBRATING

Motherhood

with the

PROPHETS

COMPILED BY SHELLY LOCKE

ARTWORK BY ANNE OBORN

CFI · AN IMPRINT OF CEDAR FORT, INC. · SPRINGVILLE, UTAH

ISBN 13: 978-1-4621-2283-7

Published by CFI, an imprint of Cedar Fort, Inc.
2373 W. 700 S., Springville, UT 84663
Distributed by Cedar Fort, Inc., www.cedarfort.com

   Library of Congress Control Number: 2018962536

Cover design by Markie Riley and Shawnda T. Craig
Interior layout and design by Shawnda T. Craig
Cover design © 2019 Cedar Fort, Inc.
Edited by Nicole Terry and Kaitlin Barwick

Printed in Canada

10 9 8 7 6 5 4 3 2 1

Printed on acid-free paper

Dedicated to

the enduring power of mothers who bring life, love, hope, and inspiration to the generations in their care; to my mother and all my grandmothers for their courage, their strength of heart, and their wisdom, which transcends the ages; and to the mothers of the prophets, who taught them by faith and example to cherish and honor the noble role of motherhood.

—Shelly

Women are endowed
with *special traits* and *attributes*
that come from a divine Mother.

—Vaughn J. Featherstone

Contents

"*My mother*
also is one of the noblest and
the best of all women."

—Prophet Joseph Smith

"Blessed
is my mother,

for her soul is ever filled with

benevolence

and philanthropy."

—Prophet Joseph Smith

"'Will mothers have their children in eternity?'

Yes! Yes! Mothers, you will have your children; for they shall have eternal life, for their debt is paid. Children . . . must rise just as they died; we can there hail our lovely infants with the same glory—

the same loveliness in the celestial glory."

—Prophet Joseph Smith

"Many of the sisters grieve because they are not blessed with offspring. You will see the time when you will have millions of children around you. If you are faithful to your covenants, *you will be mothers of nations.*"

—PROPHET BRIGHAM YOUNG

"If you *mothers* will live your religion, then in the love and fear of God *teach your children* constantly and thoroughly in the way of *life and salvation,*

training them up in the way they should go,
when they are old, they shall not depart from it.
I promise you this; it is as true as
the shining sun; it is an eternal truth."

—PROPHET BRIGHAM YOUNG

"The mothers are the moving instruments in the hands of Providence to guide the destiny of nations. *Let the mothers of any nation teach their children not to make war,* the children will grow up never to enter into it. Let the mothers teach their children, 'War, war upon your enemies, yes, war to the hilt!' and they will be filled with this spirit.

—Prophet Brigham Young

"We have committed to our care pearls of great price;

we have become fathers and mothers of lives,

and the Gods and the Holy Priesthood in the eternal worlds have been watching us and our movements in relation to these things."

—PROPHET JOHN TAYLOR

"Now crowns, thrones, exaltations and dominions are in reserve for thee in the eternal worlds, and the way is opened for thee to return back into the presence of thy Heavenly Father, if thou wilt only abide by and walk in a celestial law,

fulfill the designs of thy Creator and hold out to the end . . .

Thou wilt be permitted to pass by the Gods and angels who guard the gates, and onward, upward to thy exaltation in a celestial world among the Gods. . . .

To be a priestess queen upon thy Heavenly Father's throne, and a glory to thy husband and offspring, to bear the souls of men, to people other worlds (as thou didst bear their tabernacles in mortality) while eternity goes and eternity comes; and

if you will receive it, lady, this is eternal life."

—Prophet John Taylor

"A well-ordered, *lovely home,* in which *peace and good will prevail* is a place of perpetual delight to those who reside there, whether old or young. Where such homes exist the young who live there are not found loafing at street corners or stores, nor spending their time in gadding about from house to house and in improper company at late hours. By furnishing means of instruction, amusement, and enjoyment at home, parents can . . . tie their children to them by *bonds of affection* that can never be broken. In after years, those children will think of that home as the brightest and dearest spot in their memories; in their minds it will always be surrounded by a heavenly halo."

—PROPHET JOHN TAYLOR

"Show me a
mother who prays,
who has passed through the trials
of life by prayer, who has

trusted in the Lord
God of Israel in her trials and difficulties,
and her children will follow in the same path.
These things will not forsake them when
they come to act in the kingdom of God."

—PROPHET WILFORD WOODRUFF

"As a rule, we regard mothers as the one who gives shape to the character of the child. I consider that

the mother has a greater influence

over her posterity than any other person can have. And the question has arisen sometimes, 'When does this education begin?' Our prophets have said, 'When the spirit life from God enters into the tabernacle.'

The condition of the mother at that time will have its effect upon the fruit of her womb; and from the birth of the child, and all through life,

the teachings and example of the mother

govern and control, in a great measure, that child, and her influence is felt by it through time and eternity."

—PROPHET WILFORD WOODRUFF

"Take men anywhere, at sea, sinking with their ship, dying in battle, lying down in death under almost any circumstances, and the last thing they think of,

the last word they say is 'mother.'

Such is the influence of woman."

—PROPHET WILFORD WOODRUFF

"It is saddening to note . . . the growing inclination to look upon *children* as an encumbrance instead of as a *precious heritage* from the Lord . . . and you, . . . as mothers in Israel, should exercise all your influence against [this] and in favor of *pure motherhood*."

—PROPHET LORENZO SNOW

"You sisters,

I suppose, have read that poem
which my sister composed years
ago, and which is sung quite
frequently now in our meetings
['O My Father'].

It tells us that we not only have a Father in 'that high and glorious place,' but that we have a mother too; and you will

become as great as your Mother,

if you are faithful."

—PROPHET LORENZO SNOW

"Strive to teach your children in such a way, both by example and precept, that they will unhesitatingly

follow in your footsteps

and become as valiant for the truth as you have been."

—Prophet Lorenzo Snow

"A wife may love her husband, but it is different to that of the *love of a mother to her child*. The true mother, the mother who has the fear of God and the love of truth in her soul, would never hide from danger or evil and leave her child exposed to it. But as natural as it is for the sparks to fly upward, as natural as it is to breathe the breath of life, if there were danger coming to her child, she would step between the child and that danger; she would defend her child to the uttermost. Her life would be nothing in the balance, in comparison with the life of her child.

That is the *love of true motherhood—for children*."

—PROPHET JOSEPH F. SMITH

"The good influence that a good mother exercises over her children is like leaven cast into the measure of meal, that will leaven the whole lump; and as far as her influence extends, not only to her own children, but to the associates of her children, it is felt, and good is the result accomplished by it.

And, sisters, you do not know how far your influence extends.

A mother that is successful

in raising a good boy, or girl,

to imitate her example

and to follow her precepts through life, sows the seeds of virtue, honor and integrity and of righteousness in their hearts that will be felt through all their career in life; and wherever that boy or girl goes, as man or woman, in whatever society they mingle, the good effects of the example of that mother upon them will be felt; and it will never die, because it will extend from them to their children from generation to generation.

And especially do we hope for this in the Gospel of Jesus Christ."

—PROPHET JOSEPH F. SMITH

"I have learned to place a high estimate upon the love of a mother. I have often said and will repeat it, that

the love of a true mother

comes nearer [to] being

like the love of God

than any other kind of love."

—PROPHET JOSEPH F. SMITH

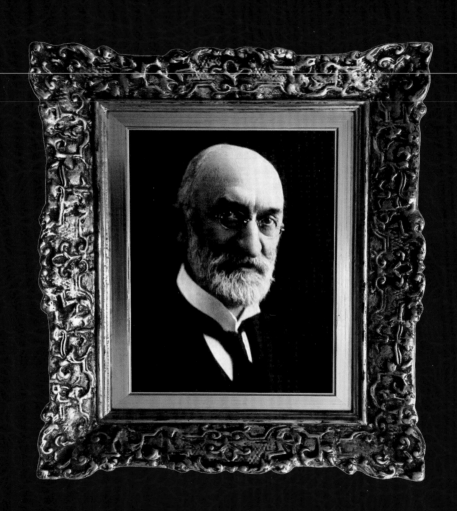

"There seems to be a *power* that the *mother possesses* in shaping the life of the child that is far superior, in my judgment, to the power of the father, and this is almost without exception."

—PROPHET HEBER J. GRANT

"Motherhood is near to divinity.

It is the highest, holiest service to be assumed by mankind. It places her who honors its holy calling and service next to the angels. To you mothers in Israel we say

God bless and protect you,

and give you the strength and courage, the faith and knowledge, the holy love and consecration to duty, that shall enable you to fill to the fullest measure the sacred calling which is yours. To you mothers and mothers-to-be we say:

Be chaste, keep pure, live righteously, that your posterity to the last generation may call you blessed."

—PROPHET HEBER J. GRANT

"*A mother's love*
seems to be the most perfect and the
most sincere, *the strongest*
of any love we know
anything about. I, for one, rejoice in it
because of its wonderful example."

—PROPHET HEBER J. GRANT

"Fathers and mothers, teach your sons and daughters the necessity of virtue.

Do not leave it to somebody else. Do not take it for granted that they understand, but in their tender years explain to them the purpose of life and guide them that they may feel that it is a

blessing from the Lord

to be members of the Church and to be sons and daughters of the Living God."

—Prophet George Albert Smith

"I want to say to our Latter-day Saints that one of the responsibilities of every married couple is to

rear a family to the honor and glory of God.

Those who follow the customs and habits of the world in preference to that blessing will some day find that all the things they have struggled for are wasted away like ashes, while those who have reared their families to honor God and to keep his commandments will find their treasures not altogether here upon earth in mortality, but they will have their treasures when the celestial kingdom shall be organized on this earth, and

those treasures will be their sons and daughters

and descendants to the latest generation. That is what the Lord says."

—PROPHET GEORGE ALBERT SMITH

"We must not forget that when we see all the richness of our lives we can't separate it from the righteousness of our mothers. It is a wonderful thing to know,

as Nephi of old, who said he was *born of goodly parents*

—he didn't say a goodly father. He was born of goodly parents, and we would do well when we think of our blessings to remember our mothers and our grandmothers and our great-grandmothers. Wherever there was a great leader in Israel there was a

great wife or mother

or both who stood by his side."

—Prophet George Albert Smith

"There are women, who, denied the power to bear children, adopt some as their own, rear them with an ability characteristic of and inherent in true womanhood, and fill the lives of their darlings with a love that only the yearning soul of such a mother can know.

Such are true mothers, indeed."

—PROPHET DAVID O. MCKAY

"This ability and willingness
properly to rear children,

the gift of love,

the eagerness, yes longing to express it in soul
development, make motherhood the noblest
office or calling in the world. She who can paint
a masterpiece or write a book that will influence
millions deserves the admiration and plaudits of
mankind; but she who rears successfully a family of
healthy, beautiful sons and daughters, whose influence
will be felt through generations to come,

whose immortal souls will exert an influence throughout the ages long after paintings shall have faded, and books and statues shall have decayed or shall have been destroyed, deserves the highest honor that man can give, and the choicest blessings of God. In her high duty and service to humanity, endowing with immortality eternal spirits, she is

co-partner with the Creator himself."

—PROPHET DAVID O. MCKAY

"*Motherhood* is the greatest potential influence either for good or ill in human life. The mother's image is the first that stamps itself on the unwritten page of the young child's mind. It is *her caress* that first awakens a sense of security; *her kiss* the first realization of affection; *her sympathy and tenderness* the first assurance that there is love in the world."

—PROPHET DAVID O. MCKAY

"I was trained at my mother's knee
to love the Prophet Joseph Smith
and to love my Redeemer

*. . . She taught me
to pray*

[and] to be true and faithful to my
covenants and obligations, to attend
to my duties as a deacon and as
a teacher . . . and later as a priest."

—PROPHET JOSEPH FIELDING SMITH

"My mother deserves a great deal of credit,

so far as I am concerned, because she used to teach me and put in my hand, when I was old enough to read, things that I could understand . . .

I had a *mother*
who saw to it that I did read,
and I loved to read."

—Prophet Joseph Fielding Smith

"Bring up your children in light and truth; teach them the saving truths of the gospel; and make your home a heaven on earth, a place where the Spirit of the Lord may dwell and where righteousness may be enthroned in the heart of each member. . . . We ask mothers

...to be lights to their children."

—PROPHET JOSEPH FIELDING SMITH

"*Mothers are the creators* of the atmosphere in the home and do much to provide the *strong foundation* for their sons and daughters, to provide them with strength when they leave the influence of their homes."

—PROPHET HAROLD B. LEE

"A mother's heart is a child's schoolroom.

The instructions received at the mother's knee, and the parental lessons together with the pious and sweet souvenirs of the fireside, are never effaced entirely from the soul. . . .

What is the mother's role, then, in the great service of the kingdom? Her first and most important role is to

remember the teaching of the gospel in the family."

—PROPHET HAROLD B. LEE

"Woman's influence can *bless a community or a nation* to that extent to which she develops her spiritual powers in harmony with the heaven-sent gifts with which she has been endowed by nature. . . . Year in and year out, she may cast the aura of her calming and refining influence to make certain that her posterity will enjoy the opportunities to *develop to their fullest potential* their spiritual and physical natures."

—Prophet Harold B. Lee

"No matter what you read or hear, no matter what the differences of circumstances you observe in the lives of women about you, it is important for you Latter-day Saint women to understand that

the Lord holds motherhood and mothers sacred and in the highest esteem.

He has entrusted to His daughters the great responsibility of bearing and nurturing children."

—PROPHET SPENCER W. KIMBALL

"*Mothers have a sacred role*. They are partners with God, as well as with their own husbands, first in giving birth to the Lord's spirit children, and then in rearing those children so they will serve the Lord and keep his commandments.

Could there be a
more sacred trust

than to be a trustee for honorable,
well-born, well-developed children?"

—PROPHET SPENCER W. KIMBALL

"*Motherhood is a holy calling,*

a sacred dedication for carrying out the Lord's work, a consecration and devotion to the rearing and fostering, the nurturing of body, mind, and spirit of those who kept their first estate and who came to this earth for their second estate to learn and be tested and to work toward godhood.

The role of the mother,

then, is to help those children to keep their second estate, so that they might have

glory added upon their heads forever and ever."

—PROPHET SPENCER W. KIMBALL

"[Mothers] are . . . the very

heart and soul
of the family.

No more sacred word exists in secular or holy writ than that of mother. There is no more noble work than that of a good and God-fearing mother."

—Prophet Ezra Taft Benson

Ten Ways Mothers May Spend Effective Time with Their Children

1. "[Take time to always] be at the crossroads when your children are either coming or going—when they leave and return from school, when they leave or return from dates, when they bring friends home. . . .

2. Take time to be a real friend to your children. Listen to your children, really listen. . . .

3. Take time to read to your children. Starting from the cradle, read to your sons and daughters. . . .

4. Take time to pray with your children. Family prayers, under the direction of the father, should be held morning and night. . . .

5. Take time to have a meaningful weekly home evening. Have your children actively involved. Teach them correct principles. Make this one of your family traditions. . . .

6. Take time to be together at mealtimes as often as possible. . . . Happy conversation, sharing of the day's plans and activities, and special teaching moments occur at mealtime. . . .

7. Take time daily to read the scriptures together as a family. . . . Reading the Book of Mormon together as a family will especially bring increased spirituality into your home. . . .

8. Take time to do things as a family. Make family outings and picnics and birthday celebrations and trips special times and memory builders. . . .

9. Take time to teach your children. . . . Teach your children the gospel in your own home, at your own fireside. This is the most effective teaching that your children will ever receive. . . .

10. Take the time to truly love your little children. A mother's unqualified love approaches Christlike love."

—Prophet Ezra Taft Benson

"*God bless our wonderful mothers.*

We pray for you. We sustain you. We honor you as you bear, nourish, train, teach, and love for eternity. I promise you the blessings of heaven and 'all that [the] Father hath' (see D&C 84:38) as you magnify the noblest calling of all—

a mother in Zion."

—Prophet Ezra Taft Benson

"A man who holds the priesthood has reverence for motherhood. Mothers are given a sacred privilege to *'bear the souls of men;* for herein is the work of [the] Father continued, that he may be glorified' (D&C 132:63)."

—PROPHET HOWARD W. HUNTER

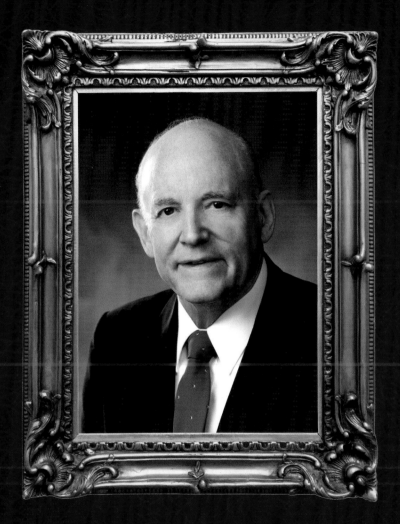

"The priesthood cannot work out its destiny, nor can God's purposes be fulfilled, without our helpmates.

Mothers perform a labor the priesthood cannot do.

For this gift of life, the priesthood should have *love unbounded for the mothers* of their children."

—PROPHET HOWARD W. HUNTER

"To be a *successful father or a successful mother* is far greater than to rise to leadership or high places in business, government, or worldly affairs.

Home may seem commonplace at times with its routine duties, yet its success should be the *greatest of all our pursuits* in life."

—Prophet Howard W. Hunter

"*God bless you, mothers.*
When all the victories and defeats of men's efforts are tallied, when the dust of life's battles begins to settle, when all for which we labor so hard in this world of conquest fades before our eyes, you will be there, you must be there, as the strength for a new generation, the ever-improving onward movement of the race."

—PROPHET GORDON B. HINCKLEY

"The home produces the nursery stock of new generations, and parents are the gardeners. In that light, I must emphasize the importance, the value, the singular

impact that women have

within the fabric of our society and in the makeup of our homes.

Mothers have no more compelling responsibility, nor any laden with greater rewards, than the

nurture given their children

in an environment of security, peace, companionship, love, and motivation to grow and do well."

—PROPHET GORDON B. HINCKLEY

"May the Lord bless you, my beloved sisters. You are the guardians of the hearth.

You are the bearers of the children.

You are they who nurture them and establish within them the habits of their lives. No other work reaches so close to divinity as does the nurturing of the sons and daughters of God."

—PROPHET GORDON B. HINCKLEY

"There is no scene more touching or beautiful than a mother kneeling with her child by his bed as she teaches him to pray. Then, arising from their knees, the little one is tucked tenderly in bed, receives his good-night kiss, and as the mother gently closes the door he hears her say, 'Goodnight, sleep tight, wake up bright, in the morning light, to do what's right, with all your might. . . .

I love you.'"

—Prophet Thomas S. Monson

"Who can probe a mother's love?

Who can comprehend in its entirety the lofty role of a mother? With perfect trust in God, she walks, her hand in His, into the valley of the shadow of death, that you and I might come forth into light. . . .

May each of us treasure this truth: One cannot forget mother and remember God. One cannot remember mother and forget God. Why? Because these two sacred persons,

God and mother, partners in creation,

in love, in sacrifice, in service, are as one."

—PROPHET THOMAS S. MONSON

"'*Mother*,' more than any other word, is held in universal esteem by all peoples everywhere. It brings forth from the soul the most tender of hidden emotions, prompts more good deeds, kindles memories' fires as they burn low, and *reminds all to strive to be better*."

—PROPHET THOMAS S. MONSON

Artwork

by Anne Oborn

References

Introductory quote by Elder Featherstone:
Vaughn J. Featherstone, "A Champion of Youth," *Ensign*, Nov. 1987, 27–29.

Joseph Smith
1. "Chapter 14: Words of Hope and Consolation at the Time of Death," *Teachings of Presidents of the Church: Joseph Smith* (2011), 171–81.
2. "Chapter 42: Family: The Sweetest Union for Time and for Eternity," *Teachings of Presidents of the Church: Joseph Smith* (2011), 483.
3. "Chapter 42: Family: The Sweetest Union for Time and for Eternity," *Teachings of Presidents of the Church: Joseph Smith* (2011), 485.

Brigham Young
1. Harold Lundstrom, ed., *Motherhood: A Partnership with God* (Salt Lake City, UT: Bookcraft, 1956), 15.
2. Harold Lundstrom, ed., *Motherhood: A Partnership with God* (Salt Lake City, UT: Bookcraft, 1956), 232.
3. Harold Lundstrom, ed., *Motherhood: A Partnership with God* (Salt Lake City, UT: Bookcraft, 1956), 233.

John Taylor
1. D. Hammer, ed., *The Works of John Taylor* (Salt Lake City, UT: Eborn Publishing, 2010), 391.
2. G. Homer Durham, ed., *The Gospel Kingdom: Selections from the Writings and Discourses of John Taylor* (Salt Lake City, UT: Bookcraft, n.d.), 284.
3. Harold Lundstrom, ed., *Motherhood: A Partnership with God* (Salt Lake City, UT: Bookcraft, 1956), 27.

Wilford Woodruff
1. Wilford Woodruff in *Journal of Discourses*, 15:12.
2. "Chapter 16: Marriage and Parenthood: Preparing Our Families for Eternal Life," *Teachings of Presidents of the Church: Wilford Woodruff* (2011), 169.
3. "Chapter 16: Marriage and Parenthood: Preparing Our Families for Eternal Life," *Teachings of Presidents of the Church: Wilford Woodruff* (2011), 169.

Lorenzo Snow

1. C. J. Williams, ed., *Teachings of Lorenzo Snow* (Salt Lake City, UT: Bookcraft, 1984), 7–8.
2. C. J. Williams, ed., *Teachings of Lorenzo Snow* (Salt Lake City, UT: Bookcraft, 1984), 141.
3. "Chapter 9: Sacred Family Relationships," *Teachings of Presidents of the Church: Lorenzo Snow* (2011), 133.

Joseph F. Smith

1. "Chapter 4: The Influence of Mothers," *Teachings of Presidents of the Church: Joseph F. Smith* (2011), 32.
2. Joseph F. Smith, *Gospel Doctrine Sermons and Writings of President Joseph F. Smith* (Salt Lake City, UT: Deseret Book, 1963), 314–5.
3. Joseph F. Smith, *Gospel Doctrine Sermons and Writings of President Joseph F. Smith* (Salt Lake City, UT: Deseret Book, 1963), 315.

Heber J. Grant

1. E. R. West, ed., *Latter-Day Prophets* (American Fork, UT: Covenant Communications Inc., 1999).
2. E. R. West, ed., *Latter-Day Prophets* (American Fork, UT: Covenant Communications Inc., 1999).
3. "Chapter 22: Teaching Children in the Nurture and Admonition of the Gospel," *Teachings of Presidents of the Church: Heber J. Grant* (2011), 203.

George Albert Smith

1. George Albert Smith, in Conference Report, Apr. 1947, 164.
2. Harold Lundstrom, ed., *Motherhood: A Partnership with God* (Salt Lake City, UT: Bookcraft, 1956), 28.
3. George Albert Smith, *The Teachings of George Albert Smith* (Salt Lake City, UT: Bookcraft, 1996), 114.

David O. McKay

1. David O. McKay, *Gospel Ideals: Selections from the Discourses of David O. McKay* (Salt Lake City, UT: Deseret News Press, 1953), 453.
2. David O. McKay, *Gospel Ideals: Selections from the Discourses of David O. McKay* (Salt Lake City, UT: Deseret News Press, 1953), 453.
3. "Chapter 16: The Noble Calling of Parents," *Teachings of the Presidents of the Church: David O. McKay* (2011), 152–61.

Joseph Fielding Smith

1. Joseph Fielding Smith, "Counsel to the Saints and to the World," *Ensign*, July 1972.
2. Joseph Fielding Smith, *The Life of Joseph Fielding Smith* (Salt Lake City, UT: Deseret Book, 1972), 56.
3. Joseph Fielding Smith, *The Life of Joseph Fielding Smith* (Salt Lake City, UT: Deseret Book, 1972), 56.